Care and repair of

RUGS
and
CARPETS

David Benardout

D1112530

For Patricia, Leon, Lisa, Hana,
Joff and Debby

Notes: Throughout this book, American terms are signalled in parentheses after their British equivalents the first time in each section they occur. In all illustrations the upperside of a rug is indicated by a dark-coloured tint and the underside by a light-coloured tint.

Editors: Michael Carter and Ray Martin
Editorial consultant: Fanny Campbell
Editorial assistant: Catherine Tilley
Art director: Elaine Partington
Art editor: David Allen
Designers: Su Martin and Jackie Wedgwood
Illustrators: Hussein Hussein and Aziz Khan
Photography: Jon Bouchier
Studio: Del & Co
Picture research: Liz Eddison

CHARTWELL BOOKS
A division of Book Sales, Inc.
POST OFFICE BOX 7100
114 Northfield Avenue
Edison, N.J. 08818-7100

CLB 4483
© 1995 CLB Publishing, Godalming, Surrey, U.K.
All rights reserved
Printed and bound in Singapore
ISBN 0-7858-0402-1

Contents

Introduction

The hand-woven oriental carpet can be one of the most beautifully made objects in the world. This is in part due to their status, for to their makers oriental carpets are not just functional coverings. Rug-making occupies the greater part of the weavers' daily life, and with their delicacy of design and artistic interpretation carpets are a vital element in their history and culture.

The art of rug-making is practised by many societies throughout the world. Most hand-knotted rugs originate in Iran, Turkey, Russia, Romania, Bulgaria, Afghanistan, Turkestan, China, India and Pakistan. A flatweave fabric known as Kelim or Gelim comes from the Red Indians of North America, from Mexico and South America.

To appreciate the artists' skill fully it is important to have an understanding of the basic principles of rug weaving. There are very few constructional differences between rugs but the variety of textures, colour and design is never-ending. It is these differences which surround the oriental rug with magic and mystique, and at the same time help the expert to establish the date and country of origin of each piece. For the good restorer the subtleties of colour and texture are important for the challenge they create to achieving the perfect repair, rather than for what they say about the rug's history, but without the sort of love and fascination for oriental rugs that prompts one to learn as much as possible about them a restorer is unlikely to achieve the high standards set by the original weavers.

As all oriental rugs are made from perishable, natural fibres it is inevitable that over the years even the best-cared-for rug will suffer some kind of deterioration, either in the loss of pile, damage to the side cords or fraying of the fringes. Although rugs often have complex patterns, the basic techniques of rug repair are not difficult to learn; what they call for is a painstaking approach, common sense and the correct guidance, but with all these the amateur can achieve excellent results.

This book has been organized into sections covering the kind of damage commonly found in old rugs, with simple and easy explanations of how to restore them. Before looking at the sections, however, you need to learn something of how oriental carpets are made.

Left: *Pakistani children weaving side by side on a roller beam vertical loom. As the weaving progresses the completed section will be wound up around the lower beam while the new warp is released from the upper beam.*

Basic rug techniques

Oriental rugs fall into two types, depending on the way they are made: knotted-pile rugs, and flat-woven or tapestry-type rugs. Flat weaving is by far the older technique and pre-dates pile knotting considerably. Pile knotting, which seems to have begun some time after 1000BC, produces rugs of a soft rich texture particularly suitable as floor coverings.

The pile of an oriental rug is usually made of spun sheep's wool, although goat or camel hair is occasionally used by nomadic tribes. Cotton and jute are used principally for the warp and weft foundations of rugs, though not for the pile. An exception to this is to be found in Turkish Kayseri rugs, which are woven completely of cotton; it has first undergone a chemical process known as mercerizing, which gives the surface of the fibre a very high, shiny finish and is thus sometimes called artificial silk.

Many fine pile rugs are made of natural silk, either in the foundation warps or in the entire rug. Such rugs are the most prestigious and sought-after of all oriental rugs. Flat-weave kelims and soumaks are nearly always made of wool, although sometimes of silk, cotton or of part-cotton.

The loom

Handmade rugs are still woven on a loom that has remained basically unchanged for centuries, which may be placed either vertically or horizontally, and is essentially a fixed frame designed to hold the foundation threads, or warps, of the rug under tension in order to allow knotting. Its length and width together govern the size of the completed carpet; a wide loom can accommodate several weavers.

The horizontal loom, or ground loom, has two bars lying parallel to each other which are held in position by stakes which have been firmly driven into the ground at each end. This type of loom is preferred by the nomadic tribes as it can be easily dismantled and carried around. The weavers working on it sit side by side on top of the completed woven pile as they progress along the warp. This explains why tribal rugs do not always lie flat, due to the varying tension created by the weavers' weights.

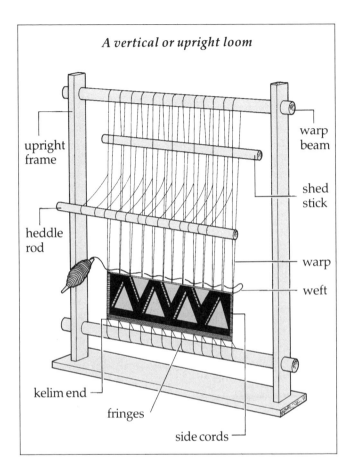

A vertical or upright loom

upright frame

warp beam

shed stick

heddle rod

warp

weft

kelim end

fringes

side cords

The vertical loom, or upright loom, is similar in basic construction to the ground loom, but it is held upright by two posts placed at either side of the beams, which make it much harder to transport. The weaver sits on a plank directly in front of the area of the carpet on which she is working. She weaves from the bottom up, and as the work progresses the plank is raised higher to the appropriate position.

For the weaving of very long carpets a variation on this latter loom, known as the vertical roller beam loom, is used. The warp threads are secured to the bottom beam and then wound around the top beam as many times as is necessary to accommodate the complete length of the required carpet. As the weaving progresses the completed section is rolled up around the bottom beam whilst the warps are unwound from the upper beam.

Pile knotting

All oriental pile rugs are hand-knotted on foundation threads known as the warp. This consists of parallel vertical threads held under tension by the loom. The number of warp threads used determines the fineness of the rug weave, and the finer the rug the more warp threads it has. To form the pile, short lengths of yarn are knotted to each pair of warp threads across the width of the carpet. When a row of knots is complete the weft is added to hold the pile in position. This is a continuous length of yarn that runs over and under alternate warps; it may be made up of one or more strands of yarn of the same, or different, thickness and texture.

When the weft has been inserted, the row is beaten down tightly against the preceding rows with a heavy

A hand-knotted oriental rug showing the complex design formed by knotting various coloured yarns.

comb-like hammer before the next row of pile is woven. Any excess of pile yarn is then cut off with a knife in one swift continuous movement after each knot is tied, and then trimmed with scissors after the completion of each row. In some cases, depending on local tradition, the pile may be trimmed to the required height after completion.

It is in the knotting process that the design is formed – by arranging the different coloured knotted yarns in various positions. The nomadic weaver works from memory, often to a design which has been handed down through many generations, but she – or, less often, he – may add small variations of her own, perhaps to celebrate a happening in the family, or possibly even just at whim. The weaver in a town or village, working in a more organized way, usually uses a pattern copying it from a design drawn on squared paper – a cartoon – where each square represents a single knot. Weavers in India often copy designs from written instructions.

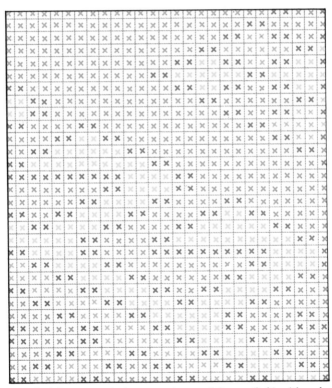

Detail of the pattern design, or cartoon, of the rug (left) with each square representing a knot.

Knots

The knots in a pile rug may be tied to the warp threads in different ways. In hand-made oriental rugs the two most common types are the symmetrical Turkish or Ghiordes knot, and asymmetrical Persian or Senneh knot. Both of these are tied around two warp threads. If the weaver wishes to proceed more quickly or make a much coarser rug she may use a Jufti knot, which may be either Persian or Turkish in type but is tied around four warp threads instead of two. There is also a knot which is tied around one warp only – the Spanish knot. This knot is tied to alternate warps in the same horizontal row and then staggered in the following rows.

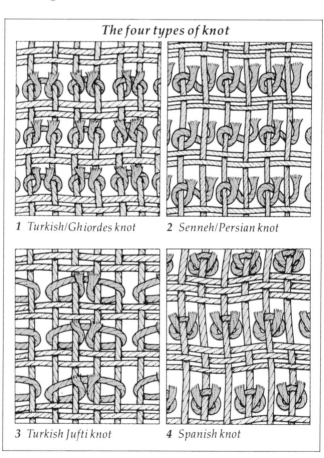

The four types of knot

1 *Turkish/Ghiordes knot*

2 *Senneh/Persian knot*

3 *Turkish Jufti knot*

4 *Spanish knot*

Turkish and Persian knots

1 *To determine the design of the knot, bend the rug back from the knots on both sides.*

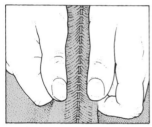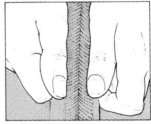

2 *If you can part the two end threads and the warp is visible,* (left) *the knot is asummetrical (Persian).*

The type of knot used has little practical significance although the Turkish knot may be somewhat more secure while the Persian knot is more easily adapted to a closely woven and denser pile. As its name indicates the Turkish knot is used primarily in Turkey, and also in western Iran and in the Caucasus, while the Persian knot is generally used in central and eastern Iran, India and China. There are some exceptions, however, and in areas of Iran where the people are of Turkish descent the Turkish knot will almost certainly be used.

In order to determine whether a rug has been woven with Turkish or Persian knots, first find a line of knots where the design is only one knot wide and also runs parallel with the warp threads. Bend the rug back from the rows of knots on both sides and see if you can part the two end threads of the knot. If you are unable to, the knot is symmetrical (Turkish); if you can and the warp is visible, the knot is asymmetrical (Persian).

A pile carpet will have a massive number of knots, so speed of operation is essential. An experienced weaver can tie between 5,000 and 10,000 knots per day, depending on the fineness of the weave and the complexity of the design.

Kelim ends, fringes and side cords

At each end of the rug, the interweaving of the weft through the warp strands is used to form the foundation of what are called 'kelim ends'. These have both a protective and often decorative purpose and are made by weaving weft threads in and out of the warp and then beating them down with a metal comb. This technique is known as flat weaving. It is often used to weave entire rugs, which are then called kelims (see below). The kelim end is, however, found on pile rugs.

The depth of the kelim end can vary from 12mm (½in.) to 25mm (1in.), depending on the origin of the rug. Some tribal rugs, however, have kelim ends of 150mm (6in.) or more.

The warp threads continuing after the kelim ends form the fringes or tassels. Some rugs have the cut warp woven into a complicated braided band at one end and the more normal cut fringe at the other.

The sides of the rug, on the other hand, are usually secured by 'side cords', also known as selvedges. These are composed of one or more warp threads (in the latter case twisted together) bound by the weft threads. Alternatively, wefts are woven in and out in a figure-of-eight through several pairs of warps.

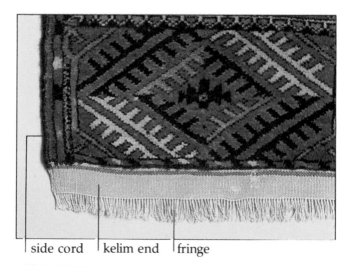

| side cord | kelim end | fringe |

Flat weaving

A kelim (the Turkish term) or gelim (in Persian) is a flat blanket-like fabric which is created by passing the weft threads in front of and behind alternate warps without any knotted pile. They are often woven on fairly narrow looms and may be constructed from two or more pieces.

The design is formed by the use of different coloured weft threads being carried backwards and forwards across the warps, not from one side of the rug to the other as a continuous thread but only as far as the pattern colour dictates. Where various colours of the design meet, a small split is formed between the two warps.

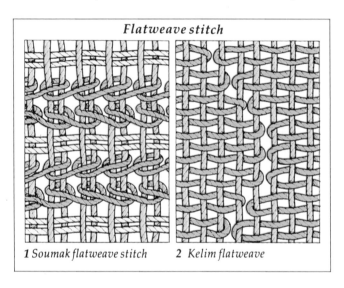

Flatweave stitch

1 Soumak flatweave stitch   *2 Kelim flatweave*

Soumak or weft wrapping is also a flatweave technique but in this case the weft is passed over and under two or four warps and then back again over two warps before being carried forward, so forming a continuous chain structure. Unlike the kelim weave, in which the pattern is usually equally clear on both sides, soumak is single-sided with the loose weft threads showing on the back. Soumaks originate from North-Eastern Iran and the Caucasus.

Kelims and soumaks are usually made of wool although they are sometimes made of silk, sometimes partially of cotton or all cotton.

Distinguishing a hand-woven pile rug from a machine-made copy

Now that you have some familiarity with the knotting techniques of an oriental rug and how the warp and weft are arranged to form the rug foundation, it should be possible for you to distinguish between hand-woven and machine-made rugs.

Machine-made copies can be impressive and at first sight one can easily be mistaken for a hand-woven original, but don't jump to conclusions until you have considered the following points.

A hand-woven Turkish rug. The fringe is integral, the cord oversewn unevenly, and the pile individually knotted.

Firstly, examine the back of the rug. If the rug is machine-made, the warp and weft will lie in perfect straight lines. Furthermore, only on hand-woven rugs is the pile actually the result of knotting on to warps. On a machine-made rug, each individual tuft can be removed from the front of the rug with a pair of tweezers.

The fringe on hand-woven rugs, as we have seen, is a continuation of the warp threads. On a machine-made rug the fringe is generally oversewn on to the rug.

Finally, the selvedge side on a machine-made rug has the overcast wool secured to the edge with a separate cotton thread similar to a line of sewing-machine stitches; the hand-woven rug has the overcast wool sewn directly between the warp threads in one continuous strand.

Remember that even the finest and most expensive of hand-woven rugs will show irregularities; it is these irregularities which make the rugs charming and unique.

The fringe and cord of this machine-made rug are secured with a machined chain stitch, and the pile is unknotted.

Dyes

Natural dyes

The aesthetic appeal of any rug depends in large part on its colours and these are achieved through dyeing. Originally all dyes were made from natural vegetable or animal substances: madder red, for example, came from the root of the madder plant; cochineal red from the cochineal insect; yellow from the weld plant, vine leaves or pomegranate peel; brown from walnut shells or oak bark; orange from henna leaves; blue from the indigo plant, and green from a combination of weld and indigo.

Vegetable dyeing has always been a very delicate and complicated process besides being very time-consuming. It is therefore understandable that in more modern times dyers have sought new and quicker methods to produce a more commercial product.

Synthetic dyes

In 1856 aniline dye was discovered in England by William Henry Perkin. The first colour was violet, or Fuchsine, and was soon followed by many others. Being inexpensive and easy to use it was imported into Persia and Turkey in vast amounts by the late 1860s. Unfortunately, the first aniline dyes were very unstable: blues turned to brownish greys, red faded to mauve, and yellows became greenish browns. The reputation of the oriental rug became seriously affected and people ceased to buy them. In 1903 the use of aniline dye was banned in Persia with very severe penalties being imposed on those who ignored the ruling.

In the 1920s and 1930s a new synthetic chromatic dye was developed in Europe. The quality of this new chrome dye was extremely good; in fact, it was more reliable and permanent than many of the original dyes and it became widely used in all of the rug-producing countries.

Natural dyes are now used only rarely in the production of rugs. However, nomadic weavers generally dyed their own yarn using natural dyes, and they continue to use natural dyes today in some areas. A current project in Turkey – the Dobag Project – actively encourages all weavers to use vegetable dyes as they produce a much more subtle colour than synthetic ones.

Left: *Careful selection of the right colours for restoration is often more important than the quality of the repair.*

Tools and equipment

1 Fringe; 2 Wools; 3 Fine
wire brush for ageing new
wool; 4 Dressmaking shears;
5 Trimming knife with spare
blades; 6,7,8 Various
weights of sewing thread and
cotton for warp and weft;
9 Pile scissors with flat
edge; 10 Fine pliers;
11 Bradawl; 12 Thimbles;
13 Tweezers; 14 Steel
pins; 15 Selection of
various needles; 16 Beeswax.

Most of the tools required for rug restoration can be found in a household needlework box or around the house. Always keep your tools clean and sharp. A blunt blade, besides causing damage by tearing at the fibres, is dangerous. It is the sharpness of the blade that should do the work, not force.

All the materials used must be of pure natural fibre only. Do not use synthetic substitutes however good the colour match, or this will, without doubt, devalue your rug. Repairs must also be carried out by using exactly the same type and thickness of fibre as the original. If the rug has a cotton warp and wool weft then those are the materials you must use. Do not improvise, even as a temporary measure. Thread should always be waxed before use to prevent unwanted knotting. On very fine rugs, if the needle point is pressed into beeswax before each stitch it will make penetration through the knot in the base of the rug much easier.

Linen sewing thread, size 18 for coarse rugs; size 35–60 for finer pieces

Beeswax, which may be purchased in blocks from a chemist, good hardware shop or wood craft shop

Sewing needles all have names and size numbers. You will find the following types and sizes the most useful: Tapestry – sizes 20 and 22; Straws – sizes 2, 6 and 8; Sharps – sizes 6 and 8

Metal thimble to be used on the middle finger. Thimbles are sold in all sizes and are an absolute must for all repairs

Tweezers with square ends

Pliers which must be small, and of good quality to be able to grip a fine needle without slipping

Scissors, either dressmaking 200mm (8in.) straight, curved pile or curved nail scissors

Wire brush of fine brass

Knife, a sharp craft knife or one with a safety blade

Cotton for warp and weft threads. You will need various sizes and colours of bulky fibre

Wool, tapestry and crewel

Small bradawl

Steel pins, 25mm (1in.)

Fringes

There are a number of ways in which a fringe or kelim end can become damaged, not least of which is the stretching and eventual breakage of the fibres caused by being constantly walked on. The first signs of damage to look out for are the untwisting and weakening of the warp threads and the breaking of the weft fibres at the ends of the rug. Should the weft threads in a kelim end actually break away, then the knots themselves are threatened, and if this is not attended to quickly, you can find that your rug is in serious danger of dilapidation.

The method of treating the repair is similar for both fringe and kelim end. There are, in fact, various methods available, and which one you follow depends on your expertise as a repairer and on the finish you are trying to achieve.

All fringes can be secured to stop further fraying by using an oversewing or blanket stitch, as in methods B and C on the following pages, but although both these methods will prevent further deterioration they will not always create an aesthetically acceptable finish. The alternative methods described here may take more time and care but they will enhance the beauty and value of your rug and increase its useful life.

However, it is important to decide on the most appropriate choice for your particular rug from the methods described, before starting any work. The main problem is, of course, how to eliminate the type of restoration which may be undesirable and then have the knowledge of how to make the correct choice of repair without causing any loss of value or detriment to the rug. This will certainly come more easily with experience but to the uninitiated it may at first seem a daunting task to reach a final decision. There are no straightforward rules, but you should not go wrong if you examine the state of the rug carefully and then read through all the alternatives with your rug in mind.

It will be found that most decisions will be simply made by using common sense. For instance, if only one small corner is missing of a rug which is otherwise perfectly sound, it would not be expedient to level the entire end by fraying out one inch of pile across the complete width, thereby losing part of the border just to eliminate the damaged area, when a small reweave of the corner would have sufficed. This adds to the value

Left: *Bokhara rug, before and after repairing a badly frayed and damaged kelim end.*

of the rug, whereas losing part of the border would have the opposite effect.

The first priority is to preserve the value of the rug, so do not rush into a repair without careful consideration. When repairing fringes it is very important to test the strength of the existing warp threads by checking to see if they are weak or damaged. It would be totally impractical, for example, to secure the ends by using Method A if the warps are weak, as within a few weeks you would find that they had disintegrated.

Remember, finally, that if after looking at all the methods in relation to your rug you feel that you do not have the skill to carry out the right one, then seek professional advice. No one wants to find they have frayed out a large proportion of border quite unnecessarily.

Removing frayed weft and loose knots

Whichever method you choose for securing the warp threads to stop further fraying you must first ensure that the final row of weft is in a continuous unbroken line across the end of the rug. If several rows of weft have become loose or frayed and the knots on them are either missing or falling out, then they must be removed completely before any securing method can be undertaken on the rug.

Using a blunt needle or bradawl and working from the back of the rug beginning at one edge, very carefully

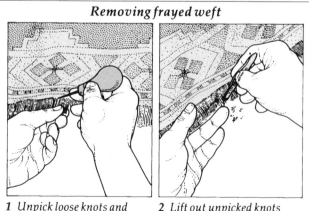

Removing frayed weft

1 *Unpick loose knots and weft with a bradawl.*

2 *Lift out unpicked knots with tweezers.*

unpick the first line of weft thread which has become loose. If the weft is still secured at both ends cut it with scissors, being careful not to damage the warp threads. Remove the rows of loose knots and weft threads until you reach the last row of damaged knots. At this stage, start picking out each individual knot in turn with tweezers, being very careful not to disturb the next line of weft. Continue until the complete line across the rug is level. Always remove only as many rows as is absolutely necessary, taking account of what the finished work will look like and the balance of the design from one end of the rug to the other.

Method A: Tying with a simple knot

Fringes over 40mm (1½in.) in length can be tied with a simple knot to secure the weft. Even on many new loosely woven rugs it may be found necessary to prevent fraying by using this method where the weaver has failed permanently to secure the final weft. Knotting three or four warps together as described below will prevent any of the loose wefts from gradually sliding beyond the end of the fringe and becoming damaged.

Lay the rug on a flat surface or table, face up, folded in such a way that the fringe is easily accessible and pointing towards you. Twist three or four warp threads together at a time, fold them into a loop, pulling the ends through to form a simple knot. Secure the knot as tight and as close to the weft thread as possible.

Tying with a simple knot

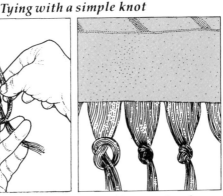

1 *Twist together three or four warp threads.*

2 *Knot the warp threads to stop loose weft fraying.*

Method B: Securing the weft with a simple oversewing stitch

This is probably the easiest stitch for the beginner and is very strong, although it is not the best-looking.

When using Method A it is not possible to secure the knotted warps very tightly against the weft threads and in time this will allow some slight movement. By comparison, Method B will make a very secure and permanent repair by not allowing any misplacement of the weft threads, although in some cases the final finish at the ends of the rug may appear to be incomplete.

Remove the frayed weft and loose knots as described on p. 22. Then lay the rug face downwards with the fringe running away from you. Use a double thickness of strong waxed thread to suit the fineness of the rug and tie a knot in the end. Hold the fringe end in your left hand (if you are right-handed) so as to be able to see the needle point coming out of the rug. Then sew sloping stitches from right to left, pushing the needle away from you, sufficiently deep to be able to catch the line of weft with each

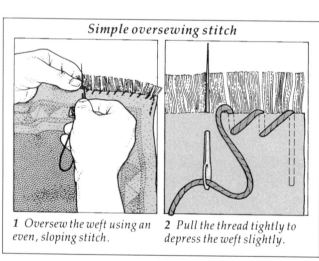

Simple oversewing stitch

1 *Oversew the weft using an even, sloping stitch.*

2 *Pull the thread tightly to depress the weft slightly.*

stitch and shallow enough not to show through the height of the pile on the front side. Space the stitches about 10mm (⅜in.) down from the weft and between every three or four warp threads. Pull the thread as tight as is necessary to depress the weft very slightly.

In some cases you may find that you need to use pliers to ease the needle in and out of the fabric.

Method C: Securing the weft with a blanket stitch

Lay the rug face down with the fringe running away from you. Work from left to right with a size 18 waxed thread of a colour to match either the fringe or pile, according to which looks better. Pass the needle through the kelim end parallel to the warps and just under the first weft. Hold a loop of thread down with your left thumb and pass the second stitch in line with the first and through the top of the looped thread. Do not pull too tightly. Continue in this way spacing the stitches evenly between every four or five strands of warp.

Sewing with blanket stitch

 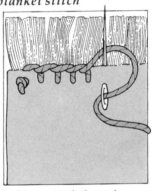

1 Sew a blanket stitch, beginning on the left side.

2 Pass a stitch through the looped thread.

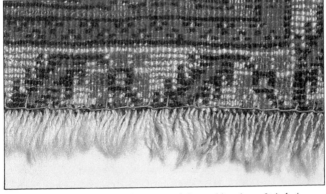

Turkish rug that was missing part of the end borders. It is being secured with a blanket stitch.

Method D: Chain stitching

This method is probably the most widely used way of joining the warps together, but is more effective on silk or cotton fringes than woollen ones because silk and cotton threads can be pulled more tightly than is usually advisable with the woollen thread. The advantage of this method over the two previous ones is that besides being very secure it will give the rug a more ornate and professional-looking finish. The disadvantage is that if it is not done tightly enough, or if the thread has not been sufficiently waxed, the complete chain can slide off the ends of the warps, especially if it is abused during normal use, such as if it gets caught up in the vacuum cleaner

Chain stitching

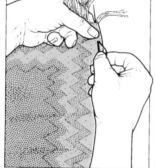

1 *Secure the side cord with two stitches.*

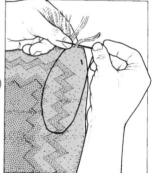

2 *Take first loop behind not more than two warp threads.*

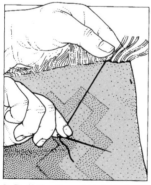

3 *Pull the thread tightly but with even tension.*

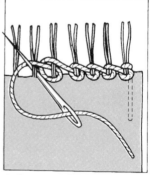

4 *Ensure each knot is pressed tightly against a row of weft.*

during cleaning or if it is too vigorously brushed.

Unpick the damaged wefts and knots in the usual way and place the rug pile upwards with the fringe running away from you. Use a single cotton/silk thread, waxed and proportional in thickness to that of the fringe. To secure the end, run the first stitch towards you from the right-hand edge and underneath the overcast wool on the side cord for about 50mm (2in.) and then back again at a slight angle. Pull the thread tightly enough so that the end cannot be seen on the surface. This is better than making a knot which would leave an unsightly lump under the side cord.

The chain stitches are formed by knitting every two warp strands together with the cotton/silk thread, in the following way, butting the knots tightly against the row of weft: pass the thread across the front of each pair of warps and hold it in place with the thumb of the left hand approximately 6mm (¼in.) above the weft. Then pass the needle behind the same two warps from right to left and through the loop held firmly in the left hand, pull to the right, parallel to the weft, to tighten.

Continue knotting each pair of warps across the complete width of the rug ensuring that all stitches are level and of equal tension. Finally, secure the thread as tightly as possible in the left-hand side cord.

Method E: Oversewing with wool

This method gives an excellent finish to a rug, particularly when part of the end border is missing and an extra line of contrasting colour is needed to complete the edge of the original design. It also gives a very strong finish to the end of the rug, particularly on short-piled pieces.

On your first attempt it will probably be found easier to begin from the top end of the rug (i.e. with the pile running down towards you, the knot being above the pair of loose ends) as when working on long-piled rugs it may be difficult, at first, to keep the ends of the tufts from being caught under the oversewn wool. It may also be found necessary to increase the bulk of the continuous strands which are placed across the base of the fringe at the lower end of the rug if part of the end border is missing and a definite contrasting line is needed to complete the finish of the rug. If the bulk is not increased the lay of the pile will cover the sharpness of the new line.

Choose a colour to match the side cord or, if the design is unbroken and it seems more appropriate, the exact

Sewing a woollen finish

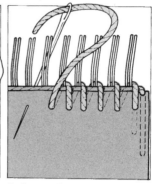

1 Secure the overlaying wool into side cord.

2 Secure the pairs of warp threads with sloped stitches.

colour of the original. You will need one or more strands of woollen thread to lay across the end of your rug as a new 'weft' and further woollen thread for stitching. Lay the rug face up with the fringe running away from you. Using a tapestry needle pass the 'weft' wool under the side cord to secure the end, and lay it across the complete width of the rug and on top of the fringe, in one continuous strand. Now wax a single wool thread of the same colour and secure this into the side cord as before. Use a simple oversewing stitch to sew each pair of warp threads together along with the overlaid wool, just below the first row of knots.

Method F: Weaving new warp threads for missing fringes

This method is quite a difficult one and is perhaps best avoided by people who do not have any experience of rug restoration.

On coarse rugs with Turkish knots and wool warps this method is not usually difficult, although on the medium to fine pieces with cotton or silk warps and Persian knots it can be extremely tough, especially on the hands, and at times it is very awkward to pull the eye of the needle through the base of the knots. As far as the value of the rug is concerned this system is certainly the best, as even an expert will not be likely to spot the repair, but it does take a great deal of practice to become proficient in it.

First, clean up the damaged warps by cutting off the loose ends, as close as possible to the knotted pile, with a sharp pair of scissors. Only prepare an inch or two at a time in order to avoid further damage during handling. Then, choose a thread which is of the same fibre and colour as the original and is also of the same physical size and texture. Place the rug face downwards with the fringe lying away from you, and using a needle appropriate to the fineness of the rug, pass the thread through one side of the first knot just above and parallel to the existing warp at least 12mm (½in.) down from the end. Return the needle parallel to the first stitch, just above the second existing warp around which the first knot is tied. Leave the new warps slightly longer than the existing warps (25-40mm/1-1½in.) and trim them when the work is completed.

Continue to insert the new warps in the same manner, remembering to make sure the thread is passed through each loop of the knots and not in between. When you have finished making new warps you should secure the fringe as explained in Methods B and D, i.e. by oversewing or with a chain stitch (pp. 24 and 26).

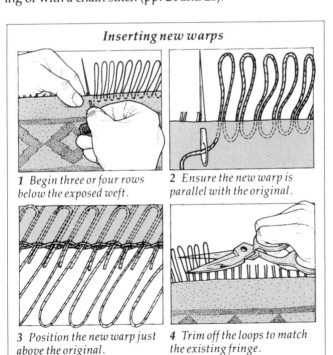

Inserting new warps

1 *Begin three or four rows below the exposed weft.*

2 *Ensure the new warp is parallel with the original.*

3 *Position the new warp just above the original.*

4 *Trim off the loops to match the existing fringe.*

Method G: Weaving and attaching a knotted fringe

This is generally the best method to use when the fringe has almost completely distintegrated across its width but the ends of the rug are still intact. An alternative is described in method F, but it is much more difficult for the beginner and far more time-consuming than this one. If you have any doubts about making such an extensive repair, seek professional advice before you start. And don't be tempted to fray out the knots to form a fringe as this will almost certainly lower the value of your rug.

To weave the new fringe you will need cotton or wool of the same thickness and strength as the original fringe. Take a length of the selected fibre 75-100mm (3-4in.) longer than the *width* of the rug and tie it between two fixed points, such as chair or table legs, with enough tension to prevent the thread from sagging. Cut up further lengths of fibre 25–50mm (1-2in.) longer than twice the *length* of the original fringe. These can be tied to the fixed length of fibre, the base strand, with a Turkish knot.

Work across the complete width of the new fringe, making sure you pull each knot tightly and pack them closely together to avoid gaps. To prevent the separate knots from sliding along the base strand and also to give added strength to the finished fringe a single strand from each knot must be tied to the next. For this you need to form the two strands into a loop and pass the loose ends through it to make a single knot.

Keep the knot as close to the base strand as possible. Having completed the new fringe, the next step is to prepare the end of the rug so that you can stitch the fringe on tidily. Remove the first line of weft thread, and with a very sharp pair of scissors cut away all the damaged warp threads as close to the knots as possible. Take this slowly, cutting not more than 50mm (2in.) of warp threads at a time so that you avoid loosening any of the knots.

When you have completed this, lay the rug face down on a flat surface with the edge away from you and with a sewing needle and waxed double thread (size 35) sew the new fringe tightly to the raw end. Sew through the base strand and 12mm (½in.) into the carpet, and back out at an angle to it. Pass the needle in and out of the same position in the new fringe but at an angle, making sure that the stitching is invisible and the knot on the fringe is not pulled out of shape.

Weaving and attaching a knotted fringe

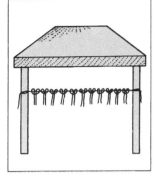

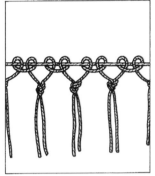

1 *Tie new cord between two fixed points. Do not stretch.*

2 *Tie strands with Turkish knots. Join them together.*

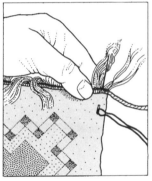

3 *Remove damaged warp threads from end of rug.*

4 *Join the fringe to the rug securing the end firmly.*

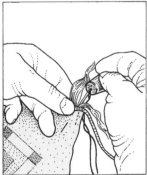

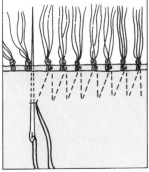

5 *Secure fringe cord tightly against the knot.*

6 *Secure fringe between each knot with sloping stitches.*

Method H: Attaching a machine-made fringe

This type of fringe is not normally aesthetically suitable for a Persian rug and should only be used if urgent attention is needed to prevent any further deterioration of the pile. However, it is certainly very useful for the more modern Chinese rug, obtainable from most large department stores. Select a fringe to match the original colour. Or, if you find you need to dye one to get the right tone, choose a good quality fast dye and remember to buy sufficient length of fringe to allow for shrinkage in the dyeing process. Do not cut or remove any of the existing flat weave or kelim from the ends of the rug as this will form a good solid base on which to attach the

Attaching a machine-made fringe

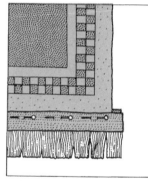

1 Hold the new fringe in position with pins.

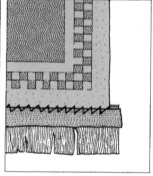

2 Attach the front side first, keeping the stitches hidden.

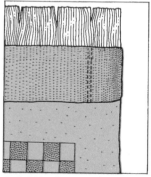

3 Fold in the cut ends, then oversew to prevent fraying.

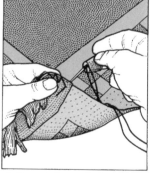

4 Do not show stitches on the front.

Chinese rug restored with a machine-made fringe to both ends.

new fringe. Lay the rug on a flat surface with the fringe pointing towards you. Insert the kelim of the rug between the flaps of the false fringing, ensuring that the face side of the fabric is on the correct side. Leave 12mm (½in.) of the fringing overlapping the edge of the rug to allow the raw ends to be folded in to prevent fraying. This will also make the completed job much neater. Pin the fringe into position on the face side only, with steel pins or tacking stitches, and make sure that none of the original fringe is showing through at the edge.

With a double waxed number 35 linen thread, sew the kelim edge of the machine fringe to the kelim of the rug with small unobtrusive hemming stitches. Work from right to left and sew only the face side – this is important. It is also important not to attempt to sew both flaps at the same time as this will cause puckering and unevenness in the fringe. Concentrate on making sure that:

(1) the leading edge is perfectly straight,

(2) the kelim is not too loose and puckered,

(3) the stitches are not spaced more than 12mm (½in.) apart.

When the side is completed fold back the end of the rug so that the fringe is now facing away from you.

Pull apart the stitching of the surplus fringe, fold back and sew into position.

Tuck in the remaining loose end and stitch into place. Make sure the stitching is shallow enough not to show on the face side. Continue until complete, finally tucking in loose ends.

Secure the end by oversewing.

Side cords

Introduction

Methods for binding and securing side cords vary from region to region. Isfahan rugs, for instance, have a single binding, some Caucasian rugs a double binding in the form of a figure-of-eight, while some Kurdish rugs have three or more bindings.

Side cords, like fringes and kelim ends, are designed to protect the rug. They are formed by binding one or more warp threads with weft threads. Most rugs also have an additional wool binding, or overcasting, as well as the weft threads.

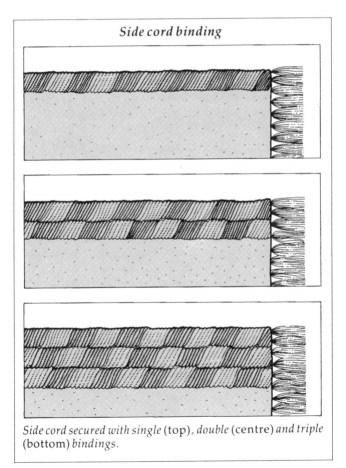

Side cord binding

Side cord secured with single (top), *double* (centre) *and triple* (bottom) *bindings.*

Left: *An Afshar rug whose side cord has been restored in the same two colours as the original.*

Simple rewooling

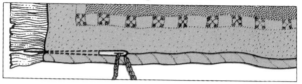

Overcasting with wool

1 Secure the end of the wool into the side cord for about 50mm (2in.).

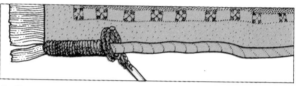

2 Oversew the cord with several strands of wool keeping the stitches close.

For simple rewooling where the edges are worn but unbroken, use a tapestry needle and colour-matching wool with a single or double strand, depending on the fineness of the rug.

Lay the rug pile side uppermost, with the edge facing towards you and, working from left to right, secure the end of the wool by running it through the side cord, parallel to the edge, for about 50mm (2in.). Then working from the front, simply overcast the cord, keeping the stitches close together to avoid unsightly gaps.

Replacing broken warps and wefts

If the actual warps of the side cord are broken they will have to be replaced before you can start on the job of replacing the wool.

First, trim the ends of the broken warps with a sharp pair of scissors to leave a clean cut.

Select a fibre of equal thickness and strength to the original warp and bridge the gap between the two broken ends of the same warp. Do not pull the new length of warp too tightly or leave it too slack as this will cause unevenness when the work is completed. Secure the thread at least 25-50mm (1-2in.) into the existing warp at both ends. It may be difficult to pull the new warp through and you may need to use pliers. Replace all the damaged warps in this way. When all the warps have been replaced the new weft threads should be added. To add weft threads to a single cord, working from the back and starting about 50mm (2in.) in from the side, run stitches along the existing weft below the pile and round the new warps of the side cord. Be sure the stitching does not alter the tension of the warps or show through on the front. With a double or treble cord the wool has to be woven over and under each band in a figure-of-eight stitch.

Now overcast the new cords, using thread that matches the original side cord as nearly as possible and closely following the stitching of the original work.

Replacing broken warps and wefts

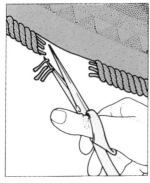

1 *Trim off the loose ends with scissors.*

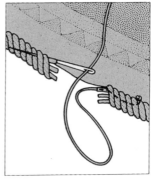

2 *Sew in a new fibre of warp to match the original.*

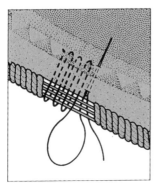

3 *Run stitches round the new warps and into the weft.*

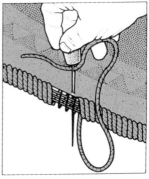

4 *Oversew the strands secure into the side cord.*

Making a separate cord

Where several feet of side cord are damaged it is best to make up a separate cord and then sew it on.

Single cord Obtain a piece of upholstery piping cord of the same diameter as the original side cord. Cut off a length 75-100mm (3-4in.) longer than the rug and stretch between two fixed hooks. After selecting the appropriate wool, wrap three or four strands around the cord. When you reach the end of each strand of wool tie off by passing back under the overcast wool. This will avoid lumps in the cord. Begin the next length in the same way.

Double cord A double or treble cord is usually flat; it is therefore necessary to bind together three or four warp strands in each band. It is not practical to stretch the warps over a long length, so use a small, square frame which will hold the warps tight for you, leaving your hands free for overcasting the wool.

Hammer in six fine nails opposite one another in the top and bottom of your frame, spaced to fit the width of the new cord. Then cut off a sufficient number of warp threads for the complete length required. Loop these over the bottom nails and tie them off on the opposite nails at the top. The threads should be pulled taut in each case, but be careful not to stretch the yarn. Overcast the wool as explained on p. 27, working from the bottom upwards packing the strands tightly together.

When you have covered the full extent of the warps exposed, remove the nails from the bottom of the frame. Untie the warps from the nails at the top of the frame and move the completed section of cord downwards. Then hammer the nails back into the same place, passing through the completed cord, one or two strands down from the top. Ensure that the nails pass between the strands and do not pierce them. Tie the loose end at the top again, and proceed this way until the required length is done.

Sewing on the new cord

First trim off all the offending edge with sharp scissors by working from the front of the rug and folding back the edge to expose the gap between the knots.

Lay the rug face downwards with the edge away from you. Starting from the right-hand side allow 25mm (1in.) of the new cord to extend beyond the end of the rug. Hold the cord along the edge and sew it to the rug using a fine needle and size 35 thread in the following way: pass the first stitch away from you just under the base of the knots, parallel with the weft, then through the centre of the cord and draw together. Return the needle back through the same spot but at a slight angle to the first stitch and then again into the base of the knots. Continue this zig-zag stitch until complete. Always take the first stitch *away* from you at *right angles* to the edge and the return stitch at approximately 45°.

Unravel the wool from the surplus cord and thread it back through the overcasting to secure it. Cut off the surplus cord level with the pile at the end of the rug. Select a yarn to match the fringe and sew it in and out of the new cord parallel to the edge to finish off the end.

Sewing on a new side cord

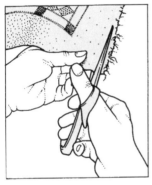

1 *Trim off the damaged area; cut between rows of knots.*

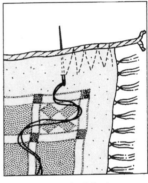

2 *Secure cord with zig-zag stitches kept closely together.*

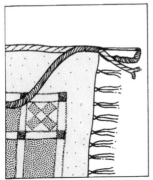

3 *Unravel the loose wool and secure it into the cord.*

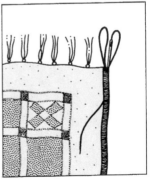

4 *Insert new warps into the trimmed off warps.*

Curling edges

Sewing and binding

In general, the more tightly an oriental rug has been woven, the more probable it is that it will curl.

When rugs curl they turn underneath at the edge. This immediately makes them look shabby, destroying the pleasing appearance that comes from an attractive pattern lying flat on the floor. Also, apart from its unaesthetic appearance, curling should be dealt with promptly as the curled edges can form ridges in the rug, and these can quickly wear and create marks and patches.

There are two basic ways of dealing with this problem. The easiest one is to sew a narrowish tape under the offending edge, being careful to ensure that the stitches are not visible on the piled surface. This method reduces the curling but it may not remove it entirely. The other procedure is much more difficult, but will keep the rug flat almost indefinitely.

When the curling is only slight, you can iron it out with a hot iron and a damp cloth. However, this is only a temporary solution, and is of no use if the curling is at all stubborn.

If you do not feel sufficiently confident to tackle either of the two remedies detailed below, then try to put your rug in a room where it will not receive heavy wear. Excessive 'traffic' on it will make the ridges worse.

Remedies to avoid

There are several other ways to try to cure curling edges – but none of them is entirely satisfactory. Because they are encountered so often, however, it is worth noting them here.

Sewing a binding strip to the inside of the edge is acceptable but not always successful, depending on the type of rug. However tempted you might be, do not try to save time by gluing a strip in place. The glue will not hold indefinitely, and you will have done more harm to the condition (and value) of your rug.

Similarly, never try to attach your rug to the floor in any way to eliminate curling.

Left: *A fine Kashan rug. This type of rug will invariably curl at the edges. Attaching tape to the edge will not improve its condition, so this rug was restored with a strong waxed thread sewn in a zig-zag manner. A fine needle and pliers were essential to penetrate the backing.*

Method A

For this you will need a strip of vinyl or leather 40-50mm (1½-2in.) wide by 2mm (¹⁄₁₆in.) thick cut to the exact length of the piled section of the rug (that is, excluding the fringes). Work with the edge away from you.

Lay the rug face upwards, and turn the edge back, then sew on the strip using a size 2 straw needle and size 18 thread. Work from right to left. Hold the strip in position with your left hand and with the thread knotted and waxed pass the needle directly through the strip and then through the back and pile of the rug. Return the needle in almost exactly the same spot and pull tightly. You are now ready to herringbone stitch the strip to the carpet back. Keep the stitches close enough together so that they will not be visible from the front, but make sure you do not catch down the pile when pulling the thread tight. Continue along the rug in herringbone fashion.

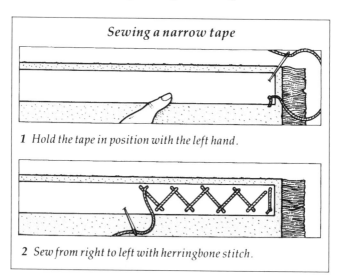

Sewing a narrow tape

1 *Hold the tape in position with the left hand.*

2 *Sew from right to left with herringbone stitch.*

Method B

This method is hard work, but is well worth the pain. Be prepared to spend two or three hours over a 2m (6ft) length.

Use a long fine needle (size 8 straw) and a double thickness of waxed size 35 thread. The finer the needle the easier it will be to use, but extreme care must be taken to push the needle in straight or it will break or bend.

Lay the rug face downwards with the edge away from you. Start from the right-hand side, uncurling the edge with the left hand. Push the needle in about 25mm (1in.) down from the edge parallel with and between the weft threads and pass it through the centre of the side cord.

Pull out the needle (with a pair of pliers if necessary) and return it back through the same spot but at a slight angle, pull the thread just tightly enough to keep the curled edge flat; if it is pulled too tightly it will have a tendency to curl in the opposite direction. Continue along the rug using a zig-zag stitch until complete. It will make it easier for the needle to penetrate the backing if you push the point into a block of beeswax before each stitch.

Sewing out a curled edge

1 *Uncurl edge with the left hand and push needle in.*

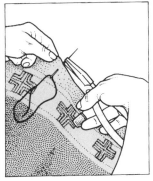

2 *Pull out the needle, with pliers if necessary.*

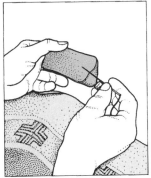

3 *Press needle into beeswax for easier penetration.*

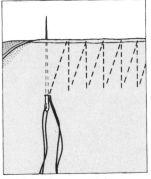

4 *Make zig-zag stitches 25mm (1in.) below the edge.*

Repiling

Knots are susceptible to damage from a variety of common household features – wear and tear from their being walked on, cigarette burns, sparks from open fires, moths, and overzealous attempts to remove sticky liquids dropped on them. When the knots get damaged or worn away they have to be replaced, in a process known as repiling. This can be a difficult and time-consuming task for the amateur, particularly if the damaged area is of any size, but it can also be a highly satisfying job.

Repiling can only be done if the warp and weft are still sound. If they are also worn through or otherwise weak then you will either have to reweave the area completely, or resort to cutting the rug down (see pp. 64-71).

A primary consideration in repiling is ensuring that the new wool is of the same texture as the original, and matches it in colour. If you cannot find exactly the right colours it may be necessary to mix various coloured strands of yarn together to obtain the right effect.

Always match colours in daylight as artificial light always has a colour bias, and this will distort the colours you are looking at. It is also important to bear in mind that the rug should be clean, or else you will be matching clean yarn to dirty, and the colour match will then be lost when the new pile gets worn or the rug is cleaned.

Before any work can commence, unpick the damaged portions of old wool. This is usually best done with tweezers. The warps and weft threads should be left clean and tidy.

Above: *The Melaz rug that has been repiled. The pile is being trimmed with a pair of scissors as the last stage of the job.*

Left: *A Melaz rug before and after repiling.*

Repiling with a Turkish knot

Lay the rug face upwards with the lay of the pile running towards you, i.e. when the pile is folded back parallel with the weft the knot is above the open end of the tuft. Begin at the left of the bottom row and make sure that the new knots are in line with the original ones.

You need a tapestry needle for this and length of the selected yarn about 450-600mm (18-24in.) long. Pass the point of the needle down between the first and second strands of warp threads, then under and around the left-hand warp and pull through, leaving 40mm (1½in.) of yarn projecting above the height of the pile. Hold down the end of the yarn with the thumb of your left hand and pass the point of the needle from right to left under and around the right-hand warp thread, below the loop of yarn, following the formation of the Turkish knot (see below). Pull up tightly between the first and second warps before moving right to the next pair of warps, changing colour as necessary.

Repeat this knotting procedure leaving the loops of pile uncut, about 40mm (1½in.) long.

When the area for repiling has been completed trim off the surplus pile with curved scissors, cutting in lines parallel to the weft. Cut down the height gradually. Remember that it is very easy to cut down, but 4mm (⅛in.) too far means another job of repiling, so be careful.

Finally, wire brush the tips of the pile in the direction of the lay, and hammer lightly to give age to the new work.

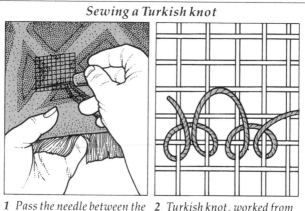

Sewing a Turkish knot

1 Pass the needle between the first and second warps.

2 Turkish knot, worked from left to right.

Repiling with a Persian knot

Repiling with a Persian knot is not quite as easy as with the Turkish knot because it is necessary to use the needle first in one hand, then the other.

Before you start you will need to work out whether your carpet has a right-hand or left-hand lay, but this can quickly be decided if you smooth down the carpet with the pile running towards you; you will find the pile has a definite lay either to right or left.

For a right-hand lay Begin in the same left-hand position as with the Turkish knot, passing the yarn under and around the left-hand warp thread as before. Then change the needle to the left hand. Study the illustration of a Persian knot and imitate this, passing the needle back over the first warp, under the second, and up again between the second and third warps. Pull tightly, and again, as with the Turkish knot, leave loops about 40mm (1½in.) long.

Repeat until complete and then trim the surface pile in the same way as with the Turkish knot.

For a left-hand lay Begin from the right-hand corner of the bottom row. Pass the yarn under the first warp thread from the left to right and pull up between the knotted row to its right. Change the needle over to the right hand and pass the needle back over the first warp, under the second, and up again through the second and third warps and pull tightly.

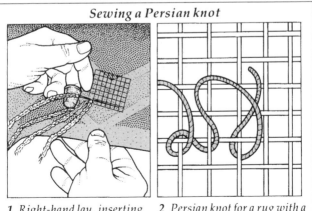

Sewing a Persian knot

1 Right-hand lay, inserting the needle with the left hand.

2 Persian knot for a rug with a right-hand lay.

Reweaving

Reweaving becomes necessary when knot damage or loss has progressed to actual damage or loss of the warp and/or weft. While reweaving can be undertaken at home it is inadvisable when the holes are particularly large, or if you are dealing with a fine antique rug.

Preliminary stages

First, examine the old warps and wefts to determine what fibre or fibres have been used – usually cotton or wool or mixtures of these. Now proceed as follows.

Lay the rug face downwards with the weft running from left to right. Clean up the loose pile on both sides of the hole by cutting through the back in a straight line between the knots and parallel with the warp threads for the complete length of the hole. Make sure the cleaned hole is angular, not curved.

Picking out the loose weft and warp of a Beluchistan rug prior to reweaving.

Left: *A fine Hamadan. This single wefted rug has been rewoven to match the original.*

Making the new warp threads

Select a suitable needle and yarn for the new warp which is exactly the same thickness and strength as the original. Still working from the back, begin at the bottom right-hand corner. Wax and knot the thread and weave in the new warp by passing the needle through the back of the right-hand loop of the original knots from three or four rows below the edge of the hole and out again just below the first row. (The first row of the original knots and wefts at the bottom and top of the hole will be removed at a later stage, so it is important that you do not run any of your new warp threads through them while you are stitching.)

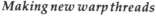

Making new warp threads

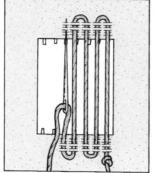

1 Pass thread through knot next to corner of hole.

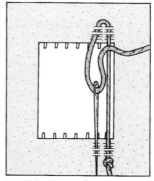

2 Take thread through knot on far side.

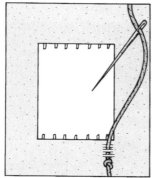

3 Continue sewing from right to left side.

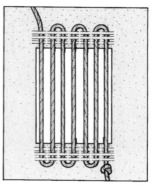

4 The hole with new warps completed.

Run the thread over the hole, keeping parallel with the original warps, making sure that the next stitch is above the first row of knots on the other side of the hole, and into the back of the second row of knots directly in line with the first stitch. Keep the needle below the surface until the fourth row. Return through the left-hand loops, remembering that for each knot you will make you must have two warp threads. Pull the thread through until it is secure.

Continue in this way, keeping each new warp below and above the surface at exactly the same point. Keep the tension firm but not overtight or you may cause distortion. Continue until all the new warps have been completed.

Picking out the knots and wefts

It is now time to remove the first row of knots and wefts at the top and bottom of the new weaving. This row is removed after the insertion of the new warps rather than before, because it is virtually impossible not to loosen or disturb the original knot whilst pulling through the new warp thread. Pick out each individual knot very carefully with a bradawl or tweezers. Now cut the ends of the weft and remove carefully, making sure you do not disturb the next row of knots. Turn the rug over to the front side and cut each old protruding warp thread as close to the knot as possible.

Picking out knots

1 Pick out knots from top and bottom rows.

2 With rug face up, trim old warp threads.

Attaching the rug to a frame

To ensure that the rug stays in a firm and flat condition during weaving, it is necessary to attach the rug to a small square wooden frame, like the one used to make up double cord (see p. 38). Proceed as follows.

Lay the rug face upwards over the frame with the warp threads running from top to bottom and perfectly square with the sides. Position the hole in the centre of the frame. With 20mm (¾in.) long carpet tacks fix the rug to the frame by nailing it onto the bottom rung, spacing the nails about 12mm (½in.) apart. Make sure the rug has a firm but even tension throughout the length of the warps by stretching it over the top bar of the frame and then nailing it into position as before. Be careful that you do not overstretch or distort the area around the hole as the newly weaved area will not then fit properly when the rug is taken from the frame.

Making the new pile

Select a suitable yarn for the weft, and with a tapestry needle build up each row to match the original by passing the yarn over and under alternate warp threads. At this stage do not cut or secure the new wefts at the side of the weaving to the original but just wrap them around the end warp and pass back again at the completion of each row; the splits along the sides can be sewn together on the back when the weaving is complete.

Choose the required colours for the pile carefully and matching the design as you work, insert the pile as described under repiling (pp. 44-7). Pack down the new wefts tightly after each row with a comb or needle making sure they are exactly in line with the original. Continue weaving alternate rows of pile and weft until complete. You can then untack the rug from the frame and, using waxed thread, sew the splits on each side of the weaving with an invisible zig-zag stitch.

Trimming and finishing

Now that you have inserted the knots, the final stage is to trim the pile to the correct height, as described on p. 46. You will find that, however well executed, the new weaving will be slightly lumpy. To eliminate this problem press on the back of the newly piled area with a hot iron and damp cloth for several minutes.

Making new pile

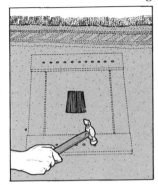

1 Tack rug to frame at 12mm (½in.) intervals.

2 Pass new weft threads around end warp.

3 Tightly pack down new wefts with needle/comb.

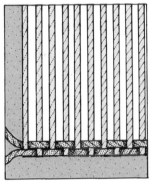

4 Continue interweaving wefts until complete.

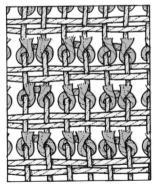

5 Repile in line with original knots.

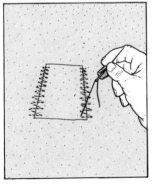

6 Unfix rug and sew up side splits with zig-zag stitch.

Patching

Reweaving and repiling becomes impracticable once a hole exceeds certain dimensions – at least for the non-professional. The only solutions remaining are to patch, or to reduce in size as described on pp. 64-71.

Whilst patching itself is not difficult when compared with reweaving and repiling, finding the appropriate patch which matches, if only approximately, the design of your rug can be difficult. Ideally the patch should come from a rug from a similar region to your own, as well as be similar in design, colour and age. This may be the occasion to consult a professional dealer or repairer to see if he has suitable patching material.

It is not possible to patch a round hole because the knots will be incomplete and, therefore, impossible to secure correctly; to make a satisfactory job all the sides of the patch have to be straight. The more proficient one gets the more complicated can be the geometry of the patch, but to begin with I suggest that you start on a simple square or oblong hole.

Left: *With this Beluchistan rug, the only possible repair is to insert a patch; the damaged area must be removed* (above) *before patching.*

Preparing the hole

Select a suitable patch slightly larger than the hole, bearing in mind that the pile of the patch will need to run in the same direction as the pile on your rug.

Lay the rug face down on a flat surface and with a strong knife or blade cut both sides of the damaged area parallel with the warps, cutting between the rows of knots, as described in the previous section on p. 49. Next, carefully unpick the rows of damaged knots and wefts along the top and bottom of the hole until they are level, cutting the ends of each weft cleanly.

Do not cut the warps at this stage.

Preparing the patch

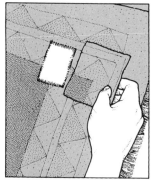

1 Check patch against hole for size and pile direction.

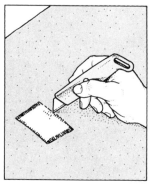

2 Cut two straight sides to hole through wefts.

3 Unpick damaged wefts and knots with needle/tweezers.

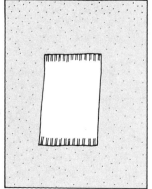

4 The prepared hole with warps uncut.

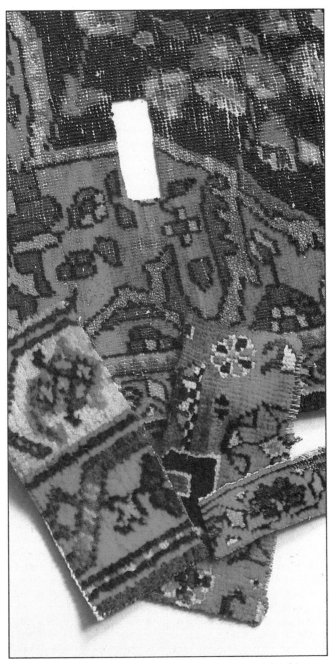

Above: *More time was spent finding a suitable patch for this Hamadan rug than actually repairing the hole.*

Fitting the patch

Having prepared the hole you need to prepare one side of the patch, cutting a straight line between two warp threads. Cut from the front with scissors, folding back the edge to expose the knots. Be careful that you cut between the knots and not through the centre of any of them.

With the pile running in the same direction as in the rug, lay the patch into the hole, pressing the straight newly-cut edge of the patch along one of the straight edges of the hole. Measure across the width and cut to size once again making sure you cut between the knots. Since the patch is unlikely to have exactly the same knot count as the original, it will obviously not line up row for row, and it is better to cut the patch a knot wider than the hole rather than narrower.

Your next step is to fray out the first two rows of knots and wefts along the top row of the patch (see p. 51). Take out the last weft very carefully so as not to disturb the next line of knots. The warps will now be protruding. Cut them off as close to the knots as possible, and cut off the ones, too, that you left in the top row of the hole.

Using a fine needle and knotted waxed thread, hold the patch firmly between the thumb and forefinger and push the needle with great care through the back of the knots parallel with the warp about three rows down. Pull the needle out between the fingers carefully so as not to disturb the knots.

Place the rug over a bottle or hard tube for support and sew in the patch in the same zig-zag fashion as already described, keeping the first stitch in a shallow line just below the back of the knot and returning the next stitch at an angle as deep as possible without showing on the front side.

Pull the thread tightly, keeping the stitches close enough together so that when the join is folded back it does not open up along the back. If the stitches are not alternated, one deep and one shallow, the patch will fray at the edges from wear. Removing the weft and sewing two rows of knots together, although more difficult, ensures a good clean join on the front side.

When this line of stitching is complete, fray out the bottom edge of the patch to the required length and cut the warps as previously described. Sew in position. Finish off by sewing both sides. If necessary you can then press the patched area with a hot iron and damp cloth.

Inserting the patch

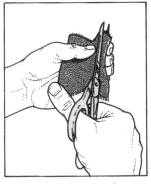

1 Fold back to expose knots; cut between knots.

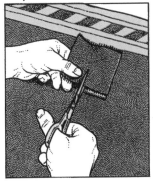

2 Cut patch one knot wider than hole.

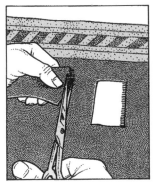

3 Trim warps at top of both patch and hole.

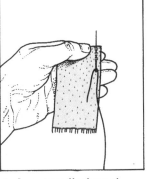

4 Insert needle through knots three rows from top.

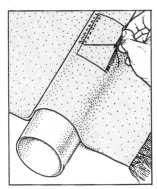

5 Sew patch into hole with zig-zag stitch.

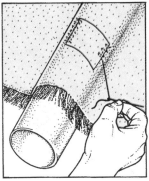

6 Sew side splits with zig-zag stitch.

Splits and tears

Splits and tears can be caused in many varying ways but in all cases the repair must be attended to as soon as possible. If they are neglected for any length of time they get much worse and extensive reweaving then becomes necessary. Moreover, once the main foundation of the rug has become damaged (i.e. the warp or weft) the knots will inevitably loosen and come out if they are disturbed in any way.

Straight unfrayed cuts

Providing the tears run parallel with either the warp or weft, they can easily be resewn together from the back with a waxed thread in a zig-zag manner.

However, any loose threads must be trimmed away as close to the break as possible to obtain a good clean finish. Even repairs to the most simple of tears can look quite unsightly, particularly from the front, if the loose strands are not cleaned away carefully before sewing starts – and you cannot remove them after the sewing has been done.

Frayed cuts

If several of the warp or weft threads have been severed but the knots have remained in their original position the foundation (i.e. the warp and weft) can be strengthened with a strong waxed thread.

The first stage is to replace the damaged warp fibres without disturbing the knots. In previous sections it has been emphasized that all foundation repairs should be repaired with the original fibre. Unfortunately, in the case of tears the main object is to avoid any further unnecessary damage, so a new fibre (waxed thread) must be used.

After trimming all of the loose fibres with sharp scissors, knot the end of the thread and begin about 12mm (½in.) below the weak area where it should be possible to get a good firm hold. Working from the back of the rug pass the needle through one side of the knot, parallel with the warp, just below the surface. Continue through the weak area for a further 12mm (½in.), again looking for a good firm hold.

When passing the needle through each side of the

Left: *This Indian carpet was badly cut* (inset) *but has been re-sewn with only a slight loss of its design.*

Frayed tears

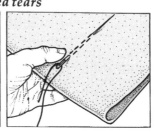

1 Trim off loose fibres with scissors.

2 Pass needle through back of knots on both sides.

knots you have to be very careful not to disturb their position in the rug. The longer and finer the needle you use the easier this will be. Hold each knot in place firmly between the thumb and first finger while pushing or pulling the needle through. If the damaged area is in the centre of the piece, the knots can only be held between the fingers by folding the rug face to face just below the weak section while supporting the rug in the palm of the same hand.

Continue across the damaged area running each stitch parallel with the warps and pulling the thread tightly enough to draw the area together but at the same time being very careful not to cause any puckering in the pieces of the rug. Finally, strengthen all of the weft threads in the same manner, but this time keeping the stitches between the rows of knots and not sewing through them.

Tears in coarsely woven rugs

In certain cases where a tear is in either the edge or end of a coarsely woven rug and there are two or three lines of pile missing, it is possible to mend it without reweaving the whole damaged area. To do this you have to extend the length of the damaged section and then rejoin the raw edges by sewing them together. The length of the cut you have to make is determined by the width of the missing pile.

Working from the back of the rug cut a straight line, parallel with the weft, to just beyond the damaged area. Pull the two sides of the damaged areas together, laying the newly-cut straight edge over the uncut frayed section until the torn portion is completely hidden. If there is a

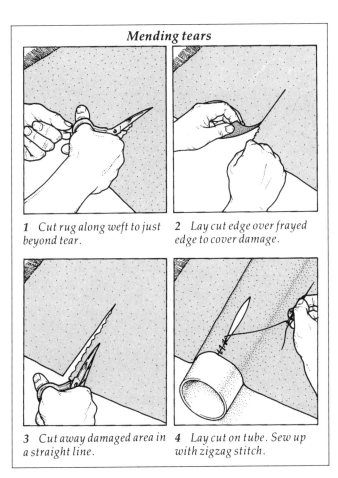

Mending tears

1 Cut rug along weft to just beyond tear.

2 Lay cut edge over frayed edge to cover damage.

3 Cut away damaged area in a straight line.

4 Lay cut on tube. Sew up with zigzag stitch.

bump or fullness at the point of the inner angle, extend the length of the cut until it disappears. Draw a line from the end of the cut to the outside edge of the rug at an angle and then from this position cut away the damaged section.

Place the split section over a tube for support and sew together with thread in a zig-zag fashion. Begin from the outside edge to the centre remembering to make the alternate stitches first shallow and then deep. Even greater care than normal has to be taken not to fray out the raw edges when handling the rug because the angled cut has also cut some of the knots through the centre. Continue back again in the opposite direction to add further strength. Press with a hot iron and damp cloth to flatten any remaining distortion.

Reducing a damaged rug

When a rug has been so severely damaged that it has come to be beyond economical repair, then it can be given a further lease of life by making it into a smaller, but serviceable, floor covering.

In most cases the reduction in size should be made in the length of the rug, that is to say, the section which is to be removed has to be cut across the warp threads. The rejoin is along the shortest length. This will also make the best pattern match as it is easier to manipulate any distortion or fullness in the rug and still keep the individual loops of each knot and all of the warp threads in line with one another.

However, sometimes a rug has been so severely worn or damaged that one has to reduce the piece by making it narrower.

Ideally, one should try to reduce the rug in such a way that it is not possible to detect the joins from the back or the front. With practice and care this is not too difficult a task, the main problem being how to work out the most suitable but practical pattern match. Try several alternatives before making the first cut. Do not be too impatient, for a wrong cut at this stage can cost many hours of work.

As a general guide to pattern-matching and cutting, study the following step-by-step instructions. Make the join in stepped stages over the width; a straight line repair will always be detected however expertly done.

Above: *A Caucasian rug badly damaged in the centre medallion. The most practical repair was to reduce the rug in length leaving only two matching medallions* (left).

Reducing in width

To produce a result which is the least detectable it is generally better, if at all possible, to make the join along one of the inner borders, making sure that not too much of the rug has to be sacrificed. However, if the shape or size of the design in the main part of the rug makes this impractical, and the join has to be through the centre of the rug, then you must be absolutely sure that the pattern matches perfectly along the total length of the join.

Removing the damaged area

Make the first cut with a pair of scissors through the centre of the worn and damaged area right through the rug from end to end, dividing it into two pieces. We will call the two pieces piece A and piece B, A being the smaller piece.

With the rug face downwards make a 50mm (2in.) cut with a sharp blade, parallel with the warps just inside the design of the inner border in piece A. Be very careful to make sure that the cut is *between* the rows of knots and not through their centres.

To find the line between the knots choose a section where two contrasting colours meet. Turn the rug over (now face upwards) and fold the pile backwards into a 'V' along the line of the cut so that the space between the knots is exposed. Continue the cut in both directions with a pair of sharp scissors. Finish the cut 12mm (½in.) from the inner edge of the border at both ends. *Do not cut across the end borders.*

Make the next cut at right-angles for approximately 50-75mm (2-3in.). Then cut at right-angles again, in the same direction as the first cut (parallel with the warps) continuing through the end border off the end of the rug. Repeat the process at the other end. You will now have removed the damaged area of piece A, and be left with little more than the borders.

Complete the cut along the last 12mm (½in.) up to the end border. Fray out this last 12mm (½in.) which is all that remains of the pile, including the last row of weft thread. Repeat the process at the opposite end of this piece of the rug.

The next stage is to cut piece B to the correct size and shape. Look at the worn section and find a point nearest to where it ends that leaves you with a complete pattern. With the scissors cut between the knots through the

Cutting away damage

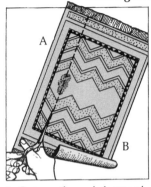

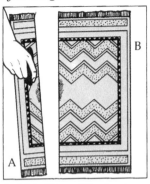

1 Cut rug through damaged area.

2 Make 50mm (2in.) cut inside inner border of piece A.

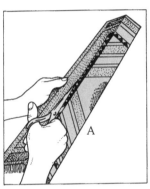

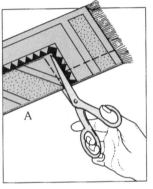

3 Turn rug over; continue line of cut.

4 Make two right-angled cuts at both ends of rug.

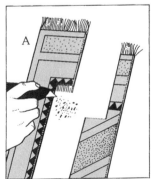

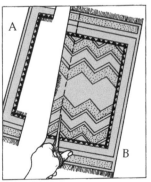

5 Fray out last of pile and weft from piece A.

6 Cut piece B to allow matching of design.

complete length of the piece including the borders, where the design of the centre field looks the most appropriate, as just determined. You will now have removed all of the worn and damaged areas.

Joining the two pieces

Place the two parts of the rug next to each other, butting up the two edges as close together as possible. Overlap the flaps of the borders from piece A on top of piece B. The line parallel to the weft at the bottom of the 50-75mm (2-3in.) frayed sections will be the finished position of the two pieces to be joined.

Measure 12mm (½in.) into the end border of piece B and cut a 50mm (2in.) line parallel to the base of the frayed warps on side A. Make sure that the cut on piece B is shorter than the frayed section on piece A, both to allow for any pattern adjustment when joining the end borders, and also to make sure you are left with sufficient carpet to complete the join. Think twice before making the cut. Remember that this area has also to be frayed out to match up with piece A. If the cut is in the incorrect position when the two sections have been frayed you may be left with a large rectangular hole in the centre of the rug.

Decide where you want to join the two parts of the border. Cut off the frayed out warps from both pieces to be joined and sew together with a zig-zag stitch, being very careful not to disturb the now unsecured knots. Also make sure that the corners meet tightly together. You will now have some surplus border on each part. Reconsider the final join of the border and then fray out the remainder of the second part (B) as necessary. Cut off the surplus of the end borders to fit. Sew the borders together, again with a zig-zag stitch, from the outside edges inwards to ensure the line of the end is square. Repeat the process on the opposite border of the rug.

Finally join together the centre section using the same zig-zag stitch as on p. 63. To ensure the rug lies perfectly flat when completed sew from the centre to the ends in both directions.

Reducing in length

Lay the rug face upwards and then fold it over so as to eliminate the damaged area in such a way as to arrive at the most suitable pattern match. Although the repair is

Reassembling

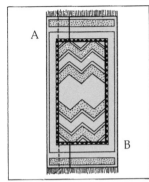

1 Match pieces A and B; overlap borders.

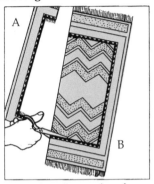

2 Cut along inner edge of border of B.

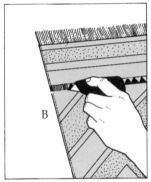

3 Fray out inner edge of B and cut wefts.

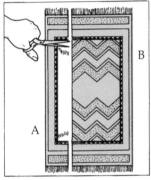

4 Trim off frayed warps from both pieces to be joined.

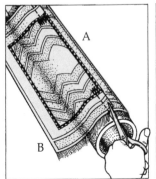

5 With rug on tube sew up and trim.

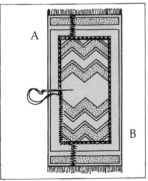

6 Make final joins of borders, then sew up centre of rug.

carried out from the back of the rug where the design is much more distinguishable, any badly faded or worn areas must also be taken into account with the overall view of the piece being the main consideration.

Mark the approximate position of the final pattern match on both edges. Make the first cut with a pair of scissors through the centre of the damaged area from one side of the rug to the other, dividing it into two pieces: A and B. Fold the pile backwards into a 'V' just inside one of the inner borders of piece A and cut with scissors along this line to within 12mm (½in.) of the position you marked for the join. Repeat along the other side of piece A. Make the next cut parallel with the weft from border to border, thereby removing the complete damaged section of piece A. Fray out the remaining 12mm (½in.) of pile up to the edge of the final pattern match. Repeat the whole process on piece B but before removing the pile from piece B, check that the pattern will match perfectly after the fraying. Then fray that end, constantly checking the match. Remove all of the wefts from the frayed areas leaving a straight line of knots.

Lay the area to be joined over a curved surface, face downwards. Take a prominent area of pattern, making sure the parts marry to ensure a perfect match. Now cut off the protruding warps for about 50mm (2in.) only on both pieces to be joined and sew them together with a zig-zag stitch. Remember to keep the first stitch in a shallow line just below the back of the knot (parallel with the warp) and the second coming back at an angle as deep as possible without showing on the front side. For the best result, space the stitches not more than the width of the knot.

Now move along a few inches to the next bold area of pattern. Cut the warps for another 50mm (2in.) and join them together as before. Progress across the rug picking out the design in stages. *Do not short cut.* Be patient. If sewing is continued without stopping to adjust the pattern match, by the opposite side of the rug the pattern will be so far adrift it will be impossible to correct it.

Finally, sew in all the gaps until the centre portion is complete. Adjust the side borders until the best pattern match is reached. It may be necessary to extend the cut parallel to the warp for the best result. Fray out as before and sew together in the same manner, making sure there is no fullness left to cause puckering. Finish off by sewing together the splits between the warps. Press with a damp cloth and hot iron.

Reducing in length

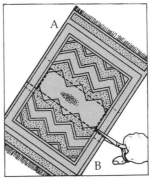

1 Fold rug to cover damage, retaining pattern.

2 Cut out damaged area to 12mm (½in.) of join lines.

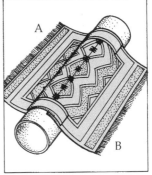

3 Fray out ends of remaining 12mm (½in.). Match pattern.

4 Sew together pattern 50mm (2in.) at a time.

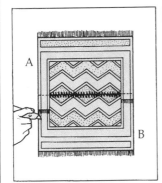

5 Match up borders, cut off border flaps and fray out ends.

6 Sew up ends and side splits of borders.

Repair of kelims

Not all the repairs that can be done to piled rugs can be produced on kelims. The problem is that a kelim does not have a layer of knots to hide stitches and joins. Any work done on a kelim is therefore more exposed. However, some of the repairs described previously in this book can be done, notably repairing fringes and edges and re-weaving, but it is difficult to mend tears or reduce a kelim without producing highly noticeable results.

Fringes

In most cases the fringes can be repaired as described in section 1. If the end of the rug is found to be very weak and fragile it may be best to secure the damaged section firmly with either an oversewing or blanket stitch as described in Fringes, Method B or Method C (pp. 24 and 25).

Repairing edges

This is normally a simple job of re-inserting the broken wefts and wrapping them around the warps of the side cords in the same manner as described for repairing the edges of piled rugs in section 2 (p. 36).

Reweaving a hole

Although the technique of kelim-weaving is simple it is very difficult to carry out a completely invisible repair. The main reason for this is that there is very little fibre to cover any loose threads. However, if you are willing to accept that the repair will show to some extent, you can reweave a section, by working as follows.

Clean up the damaged area by trimming off all the loose ends. Re-insert the missing warps as described in Reweaving (p. 50) and attach to a small frame as on p. 52. Pass the new weft threads over and under alternate warp threads, returning back again in the opposite direction at every change of colour or design (see kelim-weaving, p. 13). It may be necessary to weave in a few extra wefts to give added firmness and strength to the area. Continue the new wefts well into the undamaged area to make sure the new work is well secured.

Left: *The hole in this kelim cut across two of the colours* (inset) *but nevertheless it was possible to reweave it completely with just about perfect results on both sides.*

Daily maintenance and cleaning

One of the main causes of premature wear in rugs is lack of a suitable underfelt or padding, and a good choice of underfelt will more than double the life of a well-used rug. The available selection is vast and it is very important to choose the right underfelt for your carpet. There are various types and qualities which may be used for hard, polished or unpolished or uneven floors. Rugs laid on a fitted carpet will invariably 'walk' around the room, seemingly unaided, or become creased causing extensive damage. There are many products which are excellent for these problems and it is recommended that a recognized rug dealer should be sought for advice.

Dust and grit are like small knives and will grind away the pile if they are left unattended. Vacuuming is generally the best way to overcome this problem but it must be done carefully or you may cause more damage than the grit. Never vacuum the delicate fringed area of the rug or it will gradually distintegrate. It is advisable to vacuum lightly once a week, making sure you always leave the lay of the pile running in the correct direction. If a build-up of grit in the base of the rug is found in heavy traffic areas lay the rug face downwards on a hard surface and vacuum the back in several directions with a beater type machine. Never shake any oriental rug or beat it with a stick as this may cause immeasurable damage. Silk rugs should be lightly brushed with a soft brush in the direction of the pile and never vacuumed.

Always turn rugs at regular intervals or change their positions, where possible, to avoid excessive wear. In areas of bright sunlight move the rugs around to prevent uneven fading.

Cleaning

Cleaning should always be left to an oriental rug specialist, but there are many first aid treatments that can be used to prolong the useful life of a rug. Prompt attention to spillages is most important and wherever possible treat them immediately.

Oil-based stains such as grease, tar, fats and cosmetics should be scraped off with a blunt knife and then blotted with clean, absorbent tissue, working from the outside edge of the stain inwards to avoid spreading. Never rub at the stain as this may cause the contamination to spread and will also have a tendency to 'fuzz' the pile. Squeeze the tissue into the stained area until all the loose moisture has been absorbed and then apply a dry-cleaning solvent, obtainable from a chemist or hardware store, to complete the removal. Dab on the solution, then squeeze with clean, dry tissue. Repeat the process until all the staining has been removed. Never use water on an oil-based stain as this will allow the fibres to swell, thus absorbing the stain and making removal extremely difficult and possibly resulting in permanent staining.

Water-based stains such as tea, coffee and urine must also be blotted up immediately with clean, absorbent tissue until all the loose moisture has been removed. Make up a solution of half a pint of lukewarm water and half a teaspoonful of neutral liquid detergent for use as a wetting agent only. Lightly damp down a small portion at a time of the stained area and immediately absorb with clean tissue. Repeat several times until there is no further transfer of the stain on to the tissue. Finally, lay down a 12mm (½in.) thick layer of dry tissue over the stained area and weight it down with a cold iron or several books. Leave for twenty-four hours allowing the stain to 'wick up' into the tissue while drying, leaving a stain-free surface. Do not under any circumstances remove or disturb the tissues within the twenty-four hour period because this will prevent the continuous 'wicking' action from taking place. This simple method will remove most water-based stains if action is taken immediately. If any sign of staining remains, consult a specialist; do not try any other method.

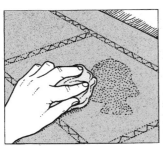 

Blot excess liquid, working inwards. Lay tissue over stain and weight with books.

Acknowledgements

Swallow Books gratefully acknowledge the assistance given to them in the production of *Care and Repair of Rugs and Carpets* by the following people and organizations. We apologize to anyone we may have omitted to mention.

Photographs: Jon Bouchier 8, 12, 14, 15, 16, 18, 20, 33, 34, 40, 44, 48, 49, 54, 55, 57, 60, 64, 65, 72; Robert Harding Picture Library 4.

Illustrations: Graham Bingham 7; Hussein Hussein 24, 25, 31, 32, 35, 36, 37, 39, 42, 43, 46, 47, 67, 69, 71, 75; Aziz Khan 9, 10, 11, 13, 22, 23, 26, 28, 29, 50, 51, 53, 56, 59, 62, 63.